God, by Man

God, by Man

OGUCHI H. NKWOCHA

ARPress

ARPress
45 Dan Road Suite 5
Canton MA 02021

Hotline: 1(888) 821-0229
Fax: 1(508) 545-7580

Ordering Information:

Quantity sales. Special discounts are available on quantity purchases by corporations, associations, and others. For details, contact the publisher at the address above.

Printed in the United States of America.

ISBN-13:   Paperback   979-8-89389-780-7
              eBook   979-8-89389-781-4

Library of Congress Control Number: 2024922842

Contents

Foreword

God, by Man
He is known as God—
God of our forefathers,
for they knew him best
and passed on the tradition.

He is called Almighty—
God Almighty,
for such he needed to be
to overcome potential opposition.

He is worshipped as royalty—
God the King,
for underlings they are
who must need be governed.

He is, of course, male—
God the Father,
for what is more befitting
to the most powerful divinity?

He is, no doubt, God—
God, by man created,
for they knew man well
and deified man's nature.

Introduction

This is the era of fundamentalism, a period marked by a furious, rather than serious, search for meaning. It is an era that is witness to the rebellion of humanity against the products of technological sophistication, because such products are perceived as too materialistic and such sophistication as senseless and godless.

Fundamentalism has taken the form of religious fanaticism whose fervor has not yet been doused by benign neglect or time. It has also acquired a tone of militancy in character with the impatience of the times. All this has transpired as humanity attempts, with a certain overcompensation, to recoil from a path perceived as leading straight away from divine precepts and right into the depths of hell.

Unfortunately, fundamentalism has only been transformed into a reversion to the same old religious traditions and doctrines that compelled the birth of scientific inquiry. The maturation of scientific methodology in turn has led to the mixed blessing of technological revolution, which at present poses a threat to the equanimity of humanity.

Those who are totally opposed to scientific progress will not admit or appreciate the great contribution of the scientific process to the advancement of knowledge and understanding. The transformation that science brought about is based on constant searching and objective testing of theories, ideas, findings, and so-called facts. This is a process that quickly (or at least eventually) exposes old myths, reexamines previous assumptions, and systematically tests all "articles of faith" for proof and reproducibility.

Knowledge and proof, however, are anathema to fundamentalist religion, where acceptance on faith alone is the one distinct mark of a believer. After all, was it not the desire for knowledge that was the undoing of Adam and Eve and, hence, of humanity to follow? The fearless and often aggressive probing of the scientific process is the exact antithesis of fundamentalism, where it is still taught that the fear of God is the beginning of wisdom.

Therein lies the problem and the danger of a return to fundamentalism. It is the problem of "that old-time religion," a song that claims that this religion was adequate for our forefathers and therefore "good enough for me" today. This is an unsubstantiated statement; there is no shred of objective evidence that the old religion was good then, let alone now, and history is the proof. Rather than reevaluate traditional doctrine and separate lore from fact, fundamentalism attempts to embrace dogma as is, dogma that is not based on truth as much as on human fancies and fantasy.

Of course, this can only lead to another vicious circle. The more fundamentalist humanity tends to become, the more the fomentation of the scientific process occurs, with science attacking nonreligious tasks that have a greater, more visible hold on humanity than does religious tradition. In such a manner, science will again force humanity to question its religious beliefs; in fear and anger and frustration, humanity will lash back by returning to fundamentalism, We have seen this cycle operative in the history of mankind, even at present.

The fact remains that with the completion of each cycle, science wins more converts, often by default, as more and more people refuse to follow blindly words whose only power is that which is lent by belief and defended by faith. These are the words of the message of religion that are an echo from the ancient past, which the present is not allowed to analyze for content and nature.

Yet with each cycle, many question whither science has led them. They are bewildered with information that they would rather not have. They are compelled along a direction that they cannot see or determine; they are held captive to a course that they care not to steer. They are not converts of science any more than they are religious converts.

In this book, basic religious tenets (the ones that form the core of fundamentalism) will be explored and evaluated for consistency and accuracy. That God who was created by man, the same one who is to be feared and not reasoned with, the one who makes people want to turn to science and knowledge—yes, that God—will be fleshed out and dethroned so that the real God may become evident.

In this book, the basic scientific process of reasoning will be directed towards ancient religious practices and beliefs. After all, why should science be banished to nongodly things? That which science has done for materialism and technology can, and will, benefit religion amply.

In the end, it becomes not a matter of choice between science and religion but simply a search for truth. It is a search that will begin in earnestness with the discovery and unveiling of the God created by man; we will find this God in traditional religion by using reasoning as our tool. This will be the purpose of this book—to roll away the barricade and to turn over an old, meaningless page.

Beyond this veil, this barricade, is God or Truth or Reality. It is for you to find out; it is your inevitable destiny to rendezvous with this—the only truth there is—with this—the only reality that is in existence. Your time is here, and you are taking the first step.

God, by Man

CHAPTER 1

Creating God

At the dawn of human consciousness, life was an intrigue, a mysterious thing of tenuous nature. Existence was a dangerous and treacherous state. There was so much that man did not know and much more that he had no control over.

Existing all around him were different states and forms, both living and nonliving, of which he had little knowledge. Mostly under the control of these other influences, he did exercise some power over a few of the others.

If man was not in charge here, who was? Somebody had to be. At first man assigned power to the most fearsome creatures, usually the most monstrous, brutal, and threatening. He would then deify such creatures and immediately begin to worship them. However, sooner or later he would discover that these creatures had just as many frailties and even greater handicaps than he himself had. In the ensuing crises of confidence, man either decided to abandon these gods (which called for a show of courage on man's part) or rationalized his continuing allegiance to them.

Next, man chose nonliving entities as the potentates of the world in which he found himself. These were not subject to the same vagaries and corruption that ravaged organic beings; surely they were more enduring, less fickle. In this manner celestial bodies were elevated to divinity; the moon and the sun, being the closest to man, garnered a giant share of this royalty.

Every group of men and women designed its own unique system of gods to suit their own peculiar circumstances and to fill the universal needs of authorship, control, authority, order, and security. These gods were inanimate objects or living things or a combination thereof. To exact and extract uniform loyalty to these gods, a cadre of subjects was formed; the priesthood has its origins here (making it one of the oldest, if not perhaps the oldest profession indeed). It was part of the responsibility of the priesthood to maintain and propagate the tradition of allegiance to the gods and to design the appropriate symbolism, rites, and rituals to legitimize such tradition.

In time, man became sophisticated in choosing and creating his gods. Those who seemed distant and insensitive to the everyday needs of man were rebelled against; this often translated into fighting against the priesthood, whose powers by now were as enormous as the gods they represented. The gods who seemed effete were dethroned and replaced by more powerful gods, usually the gods of a conquering group of army.

As his sophistication paralleled his maturity, man found himself to have more control and influence over his mental processes, and more importantly, his physical environment. The same influence formerly attributed to his gods he now could wield, albeit crudely initially, but in due course with finesse. However, because there was still a lot he neither knew nor could do, he still needed his gods. Now, they had to be upgraded; they had to be elevated above the general level of human function and knowledge.

More than that, the gods had to be humanized; not only did they have to be responsive to human needs, they would also have to be empathetic to mankind. As such, they were to be imbued with the whole range of human emotion, human mentality, and human feelings. The gods would now participate in the total range of human experience except where, by contradistinction, they were excluded as proof of their deity.

The problem with evolving deity is the loss of credibility and the erosion of authority. Man could upgrade his mentality (often with great difficulty), but it was not an easy matter to upgrade his gods without bucking tradition, thereby incurring the wrath of the gods (mainly the powerful and feared priesthood) and without presuming to usurp the functions and the responsibility assigned to such gods.

Therefore, it is not surprising that when man's needs, which originally demanded the creation of a god, have changed, man continues to hold onto that god. Man's maturation process and total evolution must continue as a matter of course, but his gods may not change much because man is still basically afraid, afraid of the many things that he has no knowledge of and no power over. Man is afraid of what or who will fill this vacuum if he rightly sacks his gods, for he knows that he cannot fill it himself.

In this manner, man created and sustained his gods. Today, a survey of various societies reveals different gods and god-man relationships at various stages of evolution and upgrading. Some relationships have been frozen in time because of the aforementioned problems of erosion of authority and credibility. In such cases the disparity between human mentality, maturation, or understanding and the assumed role of the gods is so large as to be antithetical; it engenders such great conflict that man prefers to not attempt any reconciliation. Instead, man pursues his own course with independence while remaining ever mindful of the place that he originally assigned his gods, and being cautious not to offend them.

Today man subscribes to just a few gods. The "one man-one god" attitude of ancient man was replaced by necessity and the force of socialization and institutions; these processes have not always been peaceful and have often been "ungodly," both for humanity and for the gods. During these processes, social attrition and assimilation meant attrition of deity. For as one society conquered and dominated another, the latter's gods were driven into interminable exile while the victor's gods were installed and inducted with force and imposed on all, for good or for bad.

In contrast to man's gods, who are, in effect, changing beings fashioned and designated by man to satisfy certain evolving needs, there is God. God is independent of man or man's ideas—certainly beyond man's creations, of which He knows nothing.

God is. He is not to be conceived or invoked. Man perceives a need and realizes he has no means to fulfill this need; he then invents a god to take care of it. Not this God! He is not subject to the whims and conjuration of man.

God is One. Man may create as many gods as he has kin and needs, but God remains one. One God, no more, no less! Of this oneness, division or partition is impossible—totally out of place and totally inconceivable, The responsibilities that man wants to assign to gods

3

are totally meaningless to God. There is no possibility that God could even be aware of such trust or charge. Nor could He participate in the changing desires and Perceptions of man.

Man is too busy creating and embellishing and defending and believing his gods. Caught up with his needs, his changing perception of these needs, and the means and mechanisms for their fulfillment, he will exhaust himself one day and have to rest. Then he will know God.

CHAPTER 2

Ascribing Roles to God

Having created his gods and placed them in charge, man assigned the first role to them. The system that man found himself part of must have had a beginning; the gods must be the author and force and original cause of the inception of this system.

Hence the first role ascribed to the gods was that of creator, and their first task was creation. In the history and traditions of all peoples, the gods are credited with creating the world. The gods themselves are not said to be created, except in a hierarchal system of deity where all but the supreme god is a product of the act of creation.

If they are responsible for creation, they are also in charge of maintaining order in their creation. The role of policing creation was the next charge of the gods; they had to have absolute control over the events of the world.

The gods must be all-knowing to be able to effectively exercise their powers over their creation. After all, one of the major failings of man was the lack of adequate knowledge; that had better not be applicable to the gods.

It is assumed by man that the events of the world are preordained as the world follows a course predestined by the gods. The complete plan, i.e., the master plan of the unfolding and development of creation was designed by and is in the possession of the gods. No alteration or changes are possible except by the gods themselves; only they have access to the plan.

Most important, the gods must be god-like, that is, they must be distinguished from their creation by loftiness and separated by holiness. Set apart from the rest of creation in both deportment and comportment, the gods must also be actively involved and show ongoing interest in the world.

Today, as man discovers, often by serendipity, that he can have an impact on his fate and the destiny of the world, questions are raised in his mind about the roles that he has traditionally assigned to gods. Certainly he can create different forms of "new" life; he can actively, selectively, and consciously determine the course of some events surrounding him and other entities. Where do the gods fit in now?

This question almost invariably elicits feelings of uneasiness in man. As man continues to pursue a course that takes him into the provinces originally assigned to gods, it is a question often left unanswered. The ensuing conflict never produces a single response. Instead, an ambivalent humanity is divided between those who believe and worship the gods by force of tradition but probe vigorously nonetheless into forbidden regions reserved for the gods and those who have a strong polarized stance for one camp or the other, either for the gods or for the explorers.

Since man always insists on keeping everything in perspective, his egression into divine roles is just that; he could not usurp the functions of the gods. For after all, no matter how smart he becomes, he could not have infinite knowledge. For example, he still has no way to know what the future holds. Thus the gods will always be with man, for only they can have the right and privilege of such knowledge.

Man has his problems; his gods have their tasks. But God plays not a single role in this design because God has no need to be a creator, no thought of control or order, and no desire to be holy. The nature of God does not accommodate the creations of man or the assignments of man.

God remains independent of man's musings; He simply is. Nor can He be a player or participant in the machinations of man. What God is, man has chosen not to know; therefore, man is left with only man's creations—gods that are meaningless except in the mind of man.

Whenever man decides to abandon the gods of his creation, he will make way to see God. Whenever man decides to forget man's designs, he is ready to approach God. And whenever he desires to, man will know God.

CHAPTER 3
God and Creation

In the beginning, the world was created by the gods—so is humanity taught by tradition and lore. Every distinct group of people has its own account, but the theme is the same. There was a beginning, before which only the gods existed; then, for various reasons, the world that is now evident was created.

The tradition of creation may seem logical, but this theory is one of the least defensible by those who preach it. No reason offered so far can justify creation in objective thinking, never mind that serious quarrels have resulted every time the belief in creation is questioned.

Man creates things and becomes responsible for the inception of such things; therefore, he assumes that he himself (and consequently the world) were created by some being. This being must be as superior to man as man is Superior to what man has created. This superior creator is the god of man's traditional knowledge.

Although man has imputed to the gods the qualities of ideation and manifestation (the same qualities that characterize and effectuate creation), it is important to realize that the conception of these qualities, i.e., the idea of creation, is still man's.

In essence then, man created his gods so that he can assign them the superlatives of his own functions. Man always handles these functions crudely and without finesse; it is for the gods to exhibit perfection with them.

Then one day, as it were, man stumbled upon the theory of evolution of matter and, subsequently, the evolutionary process. Kind did not, after all, produce according to its own kind in a rigid doctrine of lineage as ordained by the gods; instead, all could be traced back to something that multiplied and recombined and diversified and metamorphosed. And most important of all, it did not appear that the hand of the gods had anything to do with this process.

This discovery, while initially hailed as the proof of the demise of the creationist tradition, raised more questions. For example, immediate questions were asked about the origin of the primordial condition—that original, primal, first state from which all was derived and to which all now owed their existence. Other questions aimed to suggest the amalgamation of evolution with creation by postulating first creation, then the evolution of the created.

In the middle of this muddle is the question of the meaning of evolution, which obviously is easier to answer than the question of the meaning of creation. The ultimate driving force of evolution is neither survival nor diversity nor perfection; these are only the end-products of the process of evolution. Evolution is driven by only one factor: *Insecurity*. This is the basis and the fuel of evolution; here, the meaning of evolution can be found.

If insecurity is the basis of evolution, who does it apply to in the first instance? Obviously not man, who is only a recent arrival at the scene, a late model, a product of the process of evolution. Certainly not the gods either; man had been quite careful to impute to his gods sufficient security to protect, separate, and differentiate them from the evident weaknesses and shortcomings of man.

The evolutionists have a lot of questions to answer; in the spirit of science, they are seeking the answers by continuing their studies. The creationists have a lot to explain; in their tradition, they are adhering to their belief in their doctrines and relying on inscrutable faith. The battle is unending; humanity is in turmoil as people take sides, people change sides, and people frequently do not even bother any more.

Yet, neither the intensity of the evolutionists to prove evolution to the discredit of creation nor the tenacity of the creationists to credit the gods with creation has anything to do with God. There is no aspect of evolution that applies to God, just as there is no part of creation that appeals to God.

None of the reasons that man can think up for creation has anything to do with God. Every single reason or rationale is strictly man-made and man-originated and revolves around a need of man, which God cannot share. God has no needs that creation can fulfill; God has no needs, period.

As for evolution, the impetus is totally antithetical to God for God has no insecurities. God does not have a problem with or a desire for survival. Nor does He who is God seek diversity or perfection.

Beyond the battle ground of the creationists and evolutionists is God; beyond the creation of gods and assignment of the function of creation to the gods is God. Beyond the methodological searching and sifting process of science is God. Yet, man will not know God in the blood-thirsty scream of battle cry; man will not find God in the din of the business and activities of man, whether in creation or evolution. Certainly, man must and will experience God; he need only let go of his self-imposed encumbrances first.

CHAPTER 4
God and the Universe

One of the entities that has held the most intrigue for man is the heavens. This is the home of his gods, decorated by equally intriguing and unreachable heavenly bodies of all kinds, otherwise known as stars.

From this loft, the gods are supposed to look down on man and his world. From high above, the gods are presumed to visit on earth their blessings and their malevolence alike, depending on the situation. This is the divine command center where the fate and destiny of the world is determined.

Of course, the heavens and everything else were created by the gods. Who else could muster the resources to build such a vast system? Who else had the power and the knowledge to construct such complex and colossal works as the universe?

Even though they are just as inaccessible, two of the elements of the universe were felt to be much closer to the earth, man's home. The sun and the moon were created by the gods to mark time and rule the activities of the earth. Man has learned to adore and literally worship these two objects, ascribing to them magical powers which he taps from time to time.

The rest of the heavens functioned as a tablet, which the gods sometimes deigned to write messages for those who could decipher them. On this huge canvas they painted frightening and ominous things for man, especially when the gods were upset with man and his world for any reason.

Indeed, being in awe of the heavens has always been man's lot. Consider that his circadian rhythm is determined by the sun and the moon, that the rain from heaven either assures a good crop-yield or causes a devastating flood, or that the boom of a thunder-clap is as frightening as the forest fires ignited by the initiating lighting, all phenomena using the heavens as a medium or backdrop. On the aesthetic side, what a marvel the elusive rainbow is! Consider the emotions it elicits from the heart of man or how the moon affects us with its soft and gentle light illuminating the path and passions of lovers!

In light of man's understanding today, that awe has been stripped from the heavens somewhat, and any romanticization has been dulled quite a bit. First of all, man's conception of the heavens is not of a place; it is more of a space. It is not necessarily unreachable, since man has developed the means to get to some of its elements. Second, if it is the abode of the gods, the heavens must have been vacated at this time because no gods have been encountered in space so far.

The entities that captivated and literally held man captive are now better understood as to their nature, structure, and origin. The mysterious stars are now known to be no more than fiery balls of nuclear combustion; the sun, previously the lord and master and demigod of man, is one such ball. Like the rest, it will follow the burning course of all such cosmic bodies.

Though not as predictable, the weather is better understood; if man is no longer totally at its mercy, at least no gods are involved. Both physically and conceptually, the earth's place in relationship to the rest of the universe is also well mapped out. The riddles of the rainbow and of lightning have all been worked out.

As the myths about the universe are exploded, the credibility of the gods associated with it is seriously jeopardized. What happens now to the gods? Are they the all-powerful and prolific creators that man considered them or are they too a myth?

And what now for man? Will he abandon the belief that the universe was created by the gods? Or will he insist in believing in the reality and invincibility of the gods whom he himself created and invented in the first place to account for what seemed to him at the time unaccountable?

Humanity is divided on this issue in various ways. Tradition dies hard, so vestiges of support remain even in the camp that refuses to believe any more that the universe is the work of the gods. Doubts are also beginning to crop up among the believers. Refusing to participate in the conflict as long as it does not affect their livelihood, many people could not care less.

Whatever man chooses to believe, the fact remains that God did not create the universe. Nothing about the universe reflects the work of God; the signature of God does not exist in any sector of the universe at all.

The universe is neither graced by the shadow of God nor by the echo of the nature of God, not in the least. The universe has no means to harbor God and no credit that is befitting of God. As a matter of fact, there is nothing in common between the universe of man's consciousness and God.

Man must disband the gods whom he has created if he wants to know God; man must dismiss the universe of his gods' creation to experience God. For only when the dust settles from the abandonment of these beliefs can man focus on the only resident presence—God.

CHAPTER 5
God's Earth

One of the first acts of creation performed by man's gods was the founding of the earth. This was accomplished at (or about) the time of the creation of the heavens. The earth was soon to take on a central role in the rest of creation and in the acts of the gods.

The earth is, of course, man's home, but it is a home that he did not built himself. It was already there by the time man appeared on it. In fact, it was a completely furnished place when man arrived on it, though it might have been a little hostile initially. Man did learn the techniques of husbandry, with clumsiness at first, but later with some sophistication.

It should not come as a surprise that man should seek a landlord for the earth; doesn't every tenant have a landlord? And who was best suited to serve as landlord that the gods? The same reasoning that prompted man in the first place to create his gods applied here. And as always, the credit for creation was heaped on the gods once the gods themselves were entrenched in man's thinking.

Landlords have a lot of power; angry landlords can exercise a great deal of this power. All natural disasters were therefore attributed to the gods who were expressing their displeasure for some transgression of the tenants of earth, In this manner, phenomena like earthquakes, volcanic eruptions, and weather disturbances were ascribed to the gods.

The gods were not always in a punitive mood. After all, they did provide warmth and food and shelter on a continuous basis (even though every aspect of such provision was invested with occult danger), and water was available for thirst and cleaning and play (never mind the lurking aquatic predators).

Man naturally assumed that his earth, the creation of his gods, was the center of the universe. It was flat; at the edges one was likely to fall off. The sun, the moon, and the great constellations all revolved around a stationary earth. Because cartography was hindered by physical barriers but mainly by the mental handicaps of fear and superstition, the earth's boundaries were as yet unknown.

These days, man's thinking has been forced to change. We know the earth is not the center of the universe. Even if the idea of relative motion is invoked, the earth is still not stationary; the sun does not revolve around the earth. Moreover, the home of man is not a flat piece of real estate with drop-off edges.

As for the gods' anger translating into natural occurrences on earth, that, of course, is not so. Volcanoes, earthquakes, and weather patterns are events that can be explained acceptably even at this elementary level of man's knowledge of cosmology and geography.

The manner of the earth's origin is not much in debate in scientific circles. While not every detail is known, the working theory fits what is known so far. The earth is a product of the events that formed the stars, the sun, and other astronomical objects. All the contents and occupants of the earth derive from those cosmic events, just like the earth. Although they appear in an infinite number of different combinations and forms, the same basic elements are to be found on the earth, the sun, or a distant star as are found in man's body or man's geological formations.

It is a moot point whether these cosmic events were originally an effect of a first cause, maybe a supreme cause, maybe a divine cause, in an act akin to creation. The question of the first cause's nature (if indeed there was a first cause) remains to be answered: were the gods of man responsible or could it have been a godless first cause?

Regardless of what the answer is to that question, it has nothing to do with God. God has no need to be a first cause. For first causation is an act in time; God does not enter into time and cannot be part of an event in time. First causation, like creation, is a true act of change; God has no dealings in change or with change.

God is timeless, not in a state that is frozen in time but in a manner that is completely devoid of time (a concept that is just a little difficult for man to fathom at present). God does not change in any fashion;

man may have his rationale and reason for change, but none of that can apply to God.

God did not create the earth, and it is not God's earth either. There is nothing on or in the earth that is a reminder of God; nothing that has a relationship with God or to God. The nature and the events of the earth are completely in contradistinction to the nature of God.

Man has yet to know God, though he must. Man's preoccupation with the gods of his own making and their acts prevents the remembrance of God. These are only delay tactics; the knowledge of God, which he has always unjustifiably been afraid of, has to be his in due course without fail.

CHAPTER 6
In God's Image

In all his traditions, man considers himself the most advanced, most intelligent, and most volitional creature on earth. He regards himself as the fairest, if not the most important, of all the creations of his gods.

The anthropocentricity of man is not at all surprising. It is based, naturally, on the assumption by man that he is created in the image of his gods, his maker. No other creature is granted such a privilege; no other creature shares such a glorification.

Translated, this means that man is a true, albeit clumsy and crude reflection of his gods, in a manner that nothing else is or can be. It places man on a different echelon altogether, far above the remainder of his gods' creations.

Man's strong belief in this tradition is such that he regards himself as a caretaker of the world for his gods and as a beneficiary of the gods for all of creation. He regards himself as quite special and sees himself in a unique role.

What attribute of man is created in the image of his gods? If it is his anatomy, then his gods are not particularly in good shape. His bipedal stance and gait are quite unstable and awkward. His size and shape are not necessarily the most efficient—either for earthly living or for heaven, for that matter.

Man's physiology is not enviable either. His constant dependence on food and air for energy would indicate that if indeed he is their reflection his gods must have a voracious appetite too. Since he must rely on industrial size stores for satiation, who knows how his massive diet can be sustained? If the dominant force of human physiology, with its process of wear-and-tear replacement, applies to man's gods, too, then they have no more power over entropy than do those created in their image—mankind. What good are they as human beings? What is the essence of their divinity?

As a matter of fact, man shares his anatomical and physiological models with the other modest members of creation. There is no aspect of man whose roots cannot be traced directly or indirectly to these other lowly creatures. Indeed, there is no significant novelty in the organism known as man.

Maybe man resembles his gods in his thoughts, his communications, and his psyche. Although these are attributes and characteristics which he does not fully understand himself as yet, their manifestations are not exactly something to be proud of, i.e., something to wish on a god.

If man is created in the image of his gods, either the image is tarnished or false, or his gods are no less handicapped, vulnerable, or fallible than he is. Man is indeed not a testament that bears credit to his gods,

The fact is that man created his gods, even though he turned around and handed the title and the authority of creator to such gods. Man's gods are really created by man in his own image and not vice-versa. Man's gods reflect man's strengths and weaknesses; they reflect mankind's successes and shortcomings, Whatever limitations man has are shared equitably with his gods; whatever attributes and qualities he possesses are seen to the same extent in his gods. His dreams are imputed to his gods; his aspirations are their hopes. The death of man will be the demise of his gods.

This preoccupation with gods of his own making excuses man from recalling his knowledge of God. He is so afraid of remembering, so frightened to know God. This remembrance can only occur in time, where time is an illusion that is self-limited and can't last forever, where time cannot change anything, where time cannot alter the truth.

The truth is that God *is*. God has no creation or creations; He is one. He has no image that can be borrowed or assigned; God has no investments in anybody or any creature. He has no reflections to focus on anything, because there is nothing else but God.

Man tries to hide in time and creation from the knowledge of God, and attempts to substitute his gods instead. In due course he will stop hiding; he will stop running, for there is no power known or unknown that can prevent him ultimately from knowing God. No force or occupation nor preoccupation can bar man from recalling the knowledge of God.

CHAPTER 7
Out of Eden

It did not take much time for man to realize that the earth is a cruel place and that living in the world is a treacherous experience. No gods could find any comfort living in the conditions existing on earth; therefore, they must not have created man on earth originally. Man had to have been in a place and state where he enjoyed divine company and camaraderie at one time—at least, at the time when he was newly created.

This symbolic Eden is everything that the earth and the world are not. Eden is supposed to be man's original home, his original pristine state. Specially designed for him by his gods, it's a place suitable enough for the gods to be an acceptable rendezvous between the creator and the created.

Whatever happened in Eden; whatever happened to Eden? How did man go from Eden to earth? How did he lose the close contact and communication with his gods, and, therefore, his god-fashioned domicile? And why can't he return to Eden now?

To answer these questions, man came up with an explanation that has determined the mien of humanity and formulated the paradigm of human experience. This explanation has colored the culture of man; his traditions are thoroughly steeped in it, while his behavior is a true reflection of it "

In explaining his out-of-Eden status, man invoked the concept of sin, a concept that would forever control man's destiny and infest a man's life. It seemed like a logical answer, but its consequences are far more devastating than man could have foreseen.

In effect, man says that he must have done something wrong against his gods to have been kicked out of Eden. Yes, it was a terrible sin against the gods; in their anger and disappointment with him, the gods sacked man from Eden and banished him to hellish earth and the world that he is now accustomed to.

It is quite unusual for man to accept blame for anything; it is more natural for him to impute it to another. It is even more important for man to not place any blame on his gods. If man could find his gods culpable, this would only lead to the erosion of their authority. As such, if man is not in the place of his dreams (in Eden) then the gods cannot be at fault; man must be found in error to maintain the divinity of his gods and their infallibility.

So man sinned against his gods and was punished (in righteous indignation?) by them. As his punishment, he was evicted from Eden, never to be let in again at any time. Because of this sentence, man serves a term with hardship in a place completely unlike Eden, a place known as the earth. This is therefore the tradition of worldly living.

In essence then, no sooner was he created than man offended his creator; just as quickly and swiftly was justice done and man's punishment meted to him. And that justice was final, the punishment eternal. This is man's explanation for the fact that his condition and situation do not at all resemble the divinity that is imputed to his creator.

Why man is not in Eden with his creator is a question that will continue to plague man even if he thinks he has answered the question. Why man is so unlike his image of his creator remains a mystery although he continues to invoke his human sinfulness as the reason; this, of course, by contrast would set his creator aside.

It is a point of interest and possibly of education to note that there is another explanation. After man created his gods and set them high above himself for deification, he turned around and assigned the role of creator to those gods. Eden was created by man in the same manner that the gods were created by him. Eden was created as a protest against earth, so it could be the latter's antithesis, just as the gods were created to be all that man is not as a protest against the nature of man. Man's experience is the world; Eden is his dream. Man's concept of himself is the body; he would rather be the gods whom he dreams of, i.e., the gods whom he created.

Yet beyond Eden and beyond the world, beyond the idea of sin and past the body (and in spite of his gods) lies the true destiny of man. Of this end, there can be no escape. Though the paths may vary, they all lead to this certain end; this sure end is the knowledge of God.

CHAPTER 8
God and Original Sin

According to popular accepted doctrines, man transgressed against his gods soon after his creation. The most widely taught versions state that this original sin was disobedience. By an active act of commission and not an error of omission, man did what he was not supposed to do.

Man disobeyed a specific instruction or set of instructions given by his gods and acted in direct defiance of the rules and regulations handed to him by his creator. A serious infraction of the laws of his gods had occurred; somebody had to pay a dear price for that.

This is man's explanation for the fall from grace, as it were, the loss of direct communion with his gods. Such communion would have granted man the type of existence that his gods are believed to enjoy by virtue of their deity. That manner of existence is the exact antithesis of the experience of man.

The concept of original sin has not received any serious challenge because man can function in spite of it by choosing to ignore it or accepting it as fact. After all, one has to explain the reason for man's great suffering when he should be reflecting on the victorious living and divine attributes of his all-powerful gods.

Any law is a limitation placed on the activities of the subjects of such law; any limitation is a target for conquest, an object to overcome and override. It makes no difference if the law is formalized as tradition, rules and regulations, or just implied; it makes little difference if it is a good or bad law.

A fundamental aspect of man's nature is his abhorrence of limitations, an active aversion against any loss of freedom. Where man appears to operate within constraints, he is either trying to break such constraints or is actively being compelled by a larger force to stay therein. Most often, it is only because he perceives no limitations at all in the situation; if he did, he would immediately start scheming to eliminate the perceived restraining influences,

So strong is man's desire to remain free of limitations that he would just as soon take his own life than remain imprisoned by conditions which are perceived to be unconquerable. By the same token, he will go to war to challenge any encroachment (real or imagined) on his freedom, even at the risk of death.

Against this background, consider again the idea of original sin. If the gods were truly man's creator, they should have known better; they should have understood man's nature more thoroughly. The gods should have realized that the possibility of man perceiving any law or laws as limiting and controlling his behavior was quite high. In fact, they should have known that man is a law-breaker because he will not allow himself to be bound, not even by the laws of a deity.

Or maybe the gods knew that man was going to contravene their instructions. Maybe it was all a set-up, in short, an entrapment. Maybe they had it all worked out beforehand, and man was only destined to be kicked out of paradise sooner or later. What a terrible joke! If the gods did not know about man's capabilities, then they should not be gods at all; to not know is the special province reserved for man, not gods. If they knew that man was going to break their laws and still created man and tried to impose those laws on man, then they are at fault. A great fault, too—and theirs, not man's!

To try to explain away the above and exonerate their gods, man often uses the argument of free will. The argument states that the gods have a free will; in creating man in their image, they imparted to man the same freedom of will. Now if this were the case, the range of man's freedom could not be any more or any less than that of his gods. So if man could conceive of disobedience in his mind and exercise the will to sin, then sin and disobedience must be part of the mental set and range of will of man's gods.

If man is a creature of his gods like other creatures, he cannot make a novel contribution to creation, either mentally or physically. At its fullest extent, the sum total of man and man's activities can equal that of his gods, if he is their exact replica. At the very least, man is a small subset in the all-inclusive set of his gods. Either way, man is within the sphere that is his gods and has no means to add to or change this set.

As long as man continues to assume and teach that he is created by his gods, he will have to continue to favor this fallacious theory of original sin to explain why he is not at all like his creator. Someday he will face the inconsistency of this doctrine; at that time he will seriously question his belief in it and will realize that he has been worshipping the gods whom he created in the first place. He will realize that he made up the concept of sin all by himself.

Original sin had to do with man's desire for knowledge; he seems to have since then recoiled from this desire. Fortunately for man, the desire never died. More importantly, the desire will be fulfilled. Man will know God; that is his only destiny.

CHAPTER 9
God and the Tree of Knowledge

According to man, knowledge belongs to the gods. Whereas his gods are omniscient, man is only blessed with the knowledge of the present and an unreliable memory of the past. The knowledge of the future is well beyond man's grasp. Ultimate knowledge per se is considered well above man's capacity.

Man seems to content himself with this state of affairs. According to traditional teaching, the original sin was committed when man developed the desire to have knowledge. To satisfy this desire, he ate the proverbial fruit of the tree of knowledge contrary to the specific instructions of his gods. This earned man immediate eviction from Eden and a life-time of untold suffering and agony. This also was the origin of separation of man from intimate communion with his gods. No wonder man would shy away from knowledge.

Such a grave and drastic punishment must indicate that the offence was major. Threatened by his desire for knowledge, man's gods cut him off and practically disowned him. They branded man a sinner, an appellation that man would carry forever; he must shoulder this heavy cross and burden of guilt from the time of his birth to his grave.

If the gods created man (and in their image) why would they withhold any information from man? What is it that the gods are afraid of, and for whose sake, theirs or man's? That man has much less knowledge than his gods says more about the insecurity of the gods than it does about the ignorance of man. These gods that keep their creations in the dark must be terrified by light.

Man must have knowledge, and he won't let the fear of divine reprisal or the force of tradition deter him. Witness the peeling away of ignorance as layers of myth are exposed by knowledge under the sharp scalpel of science in this era. Witness the expanding territory reclaimed from the darkness of nescience as individuals with singular dedication light and carry the torch of knowledge in this age.

The march towards knowledge may have a setback here and there, but there is no halting it now. For better or for worse, man has, with profound seriousness, determined to have knowledge. He has improved his meager memory of the past by designing and implementing and refining record-keeping systems in which inorganic material routinely supplement and embellish the processes of his organic brain. By studying past and present events, he can predict the future

with some success.

When it comes to knowledge, man usually has no problem challenging the tradition that knowledge is the privilege of the gods. He is well aware of and quite willing to accept the consequences of experimentation required by his quest for knowledge, although these can be injurious or outrightly lethal. More important, he does not attribute these consequences to punishment by the gods.

Those who feel they do not want to partake of more of the fruit of the tree of knowledge for fear of arousing the gods' ire stand in trepidation as myth after ignorant myth is exposed. Any day now, they expect the gods to strike the scientists dead in anger; they point to mishaps as examples. When there is no retribution, they invoke the excuse of divine patience. Needless to say, knowledge would first reveal that man created these gods before it would ever cause the demise of anyone seeking it.

Even if all the successes of the scientists were multiplied a billion-fold, ultimate knowledge is still elusive. The curve of knowledge for man is asymptotic (to borrow a scientific and mathematical term); in other words, one never quite gets there, no matter how close one comes. This is because of the limitations of the scientific goal and the methodology employed to accomplish such a goal. For although the quest is for knowledge, the question, "Knowledge of what?" has either not been asked or has already been answered with prejudice.

In the final irony concerning the subject of knowledge, consider the growing child. She craves knowledge with avidity only matched by her need for nutrition. She asks to know all the *whys* and *whats* and *hows* with an earnestness that catches the adult off-guard. Like the modern scientist, she is dedicated and serious and enthusiastic about finding answers to her questions. When she matures into adulthood a sad thing happens. She is no longer interested in learning more and must be compelled by the necessity of survival to increase her knowledge. She now has a mortal fear of knowledge. This is not a maturation process; it is the process of atavism!

Assigning knowledge to the gods will not provide cover for man forever; sooner or later he will have to come out of hiding from this folly. When he does, God will be there as He has always been, and man will gain knowledge of Him. Science needs to ask the right questions and maintain an open mind about the answer. When it does, God will be there; God is the knowledge that awaits the discovery of science.

CHAPTER 10
Life on Earth

Life was created soon after the earth was made. There was something magical about life: it could change drastically into a state of nothingness. This was quite unlike the other matter of earth; the rocks, for example, never ceased to be—unless they were swallowed up by an earthquake or vaporized by the inferno of a volcanic eruption, but it was not quite the same.

Tradition has it that the gods created living things with a difference. After fashioning them out of the dust of the earth, they breathed a "breath of life" into them, thus giving them the quality of life. They then became living as opposed to the lump of earth that is a rock.

By this tradition, it is not very clear who received this breath of life. Man certainly did—that is how he was created; animals must have, too because they breathe. Since the lack of obvious breathing anatomy would have suggested that they did not breathe, similarly endowed species must have been few by man's reckoning. Fish, for example— who would have guessed initially that they needed oxygen?

And what about the trees? They were living alright, but they appeared not to be breathing. The insects and the crawly things, especially reptiles, and the winged creatures, small and large, they were all alive, but it was never said that they got the breath of life.

This breath of life was quite special; all its recipients had a glow and twinkle in their eyes. In fact, it could be said that when that glow was gone, the breath also was gone—and so was life. So intriguing is this glow that the eyes became an organ of both expression and captivation. One could read the state and level of life in the eyes; one could also mesmerize and hypnotize another being with various gazes.

As extraordinary and unique as it was enigmatic, life could not be defined: it was not one particular thing or the other. However, the end of life was quite definite, often preceded by dramatic events that were irreversible. It was indeed a gift that only the gods could give because only they could understand it in its entirety.

It was indeed only the gods who did give the gift of life. Also, it was certainly they alone who took it away when they deemed it necessary. Of all the gifts of man's gods, life was supreme—the most special, valued, and coveted blessing. It was also the ultimate means of controlling the living things created by man's gods, including man himself.

Biology, microbiology, respiratory physiology, and general physiology have opened man's mind to a lot of factual knowledge about life. These sciences can better define the functions of life than they can its absence or presence. Common sense (or is it general maturity?) has taught man just as much about life as the exacting methodology of the sciences.

More things depend on the "breath of life" for their existence that were originally known to man. The "breath of life" is no more than a gas or combination of gases which an organism needs to produce energy for living activities and reproduction. Primarily, it turns out to be oxygen for a great majority of living things and carbon dioxide for most green plants. These gases are used to sustain and support rather than to initiate life.

Certain conditions are not conducive to life; death is the swift end-result if those life-sustaining conditions start varying. If there is time to correct these conditions, life may yet be saved; otherwise, life becomes Overwhelmed and is terminated.

In daring experiments, scientists have attempted to simulate the state existing on earth prior to the creation of life and have succeeded in showing that given the right conditions, the molecular basis of biological life will spontaneously form. Such a molecule or molecules would then depend on the forces of evolution to determine its course of development into simple structures or the complexity that is man.

Obviously, in light of such scientific findings, humanity has begun to question the traditional teaching of life as a gift of the gods. There is a subconscious search for that esoteric, evanescent breath that is altogether animating (other than the common gas with which man is acquainted). Life is so tenuous; neither science nor the gods have the answer.

Even as he writhes in the conflict so engendered, man grapples with these issues. Even a seeming answer leads to more questions, as new questions demand more answers in a never-ending cycle.

God has no role to play in life as it is conceived of by man, earthly life means nothing to God at all. It is just as well that such life is attributed to man's gods, those nonexistent species developed by man to take up the gaps in his knowledge.

God is Life; God is the meaning, substance, essence, and nature of Life. This Life is not found on earth or in any of man's creations at all because it cannot be created; it is incompatible with the state called earth or the state known as man. Because God merely is, Life is.

Man must give up his concepts of life as he knows and understands it on earth. He must stop believing in it and in the gods to whom he has assigned the creation of life. Then he will begin to glimpse the only reality that is Life—that is God.

CHAPTER 11
God and Ecology

By the time man finally started to reflect on his feeding behavior and needs, he was no longer a creature of instinct. No longer just another hunter and food-gatherer completely obsessed with the next kill and the next meal, he stopped being a slave driven solely by the need to satisfy seemingly insatiable hunger.

Man realized by now that food was necessary to provide energy and sustain life as he knew it. Gustatory pleasure was just an ancillary delight (the icing on the cake as it were) and, perhaps, provided an irresistible excitement that compelled man to keep reexperiencing it.

Man also realized that food was not necessarily plentiful; in fact, the same food items were just as popular with one species as with another. The result of this situation was the state of fierce competition where only the winners survived. Besides, there was also predation, from which no species, not even man, was free.

It was becoming clear by this time that man had established himself far above other elements of creation. He alone had more control over his fate and actions than the rest of the species. He demonstrated great skill in the procurement of food and developed an omnivorous palate.

Yet, man could neither predict the harvest nor the bounty nor the spoils. Often he could not even protect himself effectively from falling prey and devolving to food for other species or for another of his own species for that matter. Somebody other than man had to be in ultimate control.

The gods of man had to be in charge overall. They were responsible for doling out food. They also gave the authority to man, their most favored creation, to use for food anything that gave man pleasure. If it creeped or crawled or flew or swam, it belonged to man for food. When it moved, it had a potential to land on man's dinner table; when it did not move, it had the same chance of being eaten by man.

To express his gratitude to his gods for his position and power in the food chain, man shares his food with the gods; in fact, he is expected to prepare and present a dish of the choicest portion of his food to his gods. Around this idea has arisen an elaborate ritual of sacrifice, thanksgiving, and burnt offerings, all designed to please the gods. When the gods are pleased, the result is surfeit; when they are unimpressed with the sacrifice, famine is sure to strike, and means of appeasement must be sought.

At this moment in history, ecology has better elucidated the role of man in the food cycle and his place in the food pyramid. He no longer recklessly Samples or uses everything edible On earth as food for his table. He is not particularly privileged when it comes to food; his prowess in the area of food gathering is the result of expertise and the advanced knowledge of tools. If he misuses it, he and all of creation will suffer.

For all his sophistication, man exhibits great ignorance of his role in ecology. Most living things behave as part of the ecology; they live and die to benefit the ecosystem. In death, for example, man tries to rob the ecosystem of his organic body, often by making it inaccessible to other elements of the system. He frequently ignores the balance in the system for short-sighted, often short-lived gains.

As for the role of the gods in ecology, evidence is lacking that they control it in any way. The world has poor tolerance for a temperamental god who would bless here and curse there in terms of food abundance or famishment. The world has even less respect for the god who demands any form of appeasement, the god who enjoys the smell of barbecue.

Why would any god, with all the resources Presumably available to it, design a system where One species would have to devour another to survive? What is so good about a predatory system where blood is the currency of existence? Life at the expense of another is merely death delayed but death nonetheless. It has no appeal.

Man has created his gods and attributed a great deal of power to them, but he claims and believes in the independent existence and intrinsic power of such gods. He denies his role as the originator of the gods whom he worships. If he subjects his assumptions and beliefs to reason (as he has done in other areas, for example, science), he will see the truth of it all.

When man chooses to reevaluate his beliefs is up to him. For it is not a question of *if*, as much as *when*, because he surely must. On that day, man will meet his destiny and consummate his existence; he will know God.

CHAPTER 12
God and the Chosen

Lost in the myriads of forms that represent the totality of creation, man has no greater desire, no need more pressing, than to be special. He needs to be reassured that the overwhelming size and numbers of other elements of creation do not crush him into total insignificance.

Even within his own species, man still has a need to be treated not so much deferentially as differently. It is quite important to him that he is set apart in some manner from the rest of the crowd. If necessary, he would go out of his way to get this treatment.

In his attempt to legitimize his feeling of specialness, man has assigned the gods the role of originating the order of the chosen, so to speak. Typically, the chosen are an ethnic group (or subdivision thereof) or a group of people bonded by political or doctrinal leanings. They are picked usually because they have found favor with the gods at a time and place when others are found lacking.

The chosen consider themselves the only heirs of the gods. They boast perquisites that are the envy of others. Having found that specialness from which others are excluded, they are proud of and often arrogant about this heritage. It is the ultimate mark of distinction and bears the seal of divinity.

Who are the non-chosen, and where is their place? Who are the not-so-special, and what is their role? In a world created by the gods, where do those who do not find favor with the gods go? If man was created in the image of the gods, then what kind of an image belongs to the one who is passed over?

Being what he is, man will not be outdone. It is only the rare group of humans who does not consider itself chosen, Each group accomplishes this by having its own set of gods or tracing a lineage (no matter how tortuous) to the chosen people of an accepted god or gods. After all, everybody must feel special; everybody has to be special.

However, specialness, like all human desires and attributes, is perceived to be in short supply; after all, if everyone became special, where then is specialness? Specialness also lends itself to relativity and comparison. One group will always try to be more special than the others with obvious implications. The most horrifying fact is that man will go to war just to defend his specialness.

Today, the world is teeming with special people, the chosen of all races and nations. Yet, there is nothing intrinsic about their status. If one believes he is chosen, he acts in that manner. It is a belief, a custom for him, but not a reality. Alas, he takes his "chosenness" too seriously and must ostracize his brother to prove it. In so doing, he lays the foundation for an adversarial system. By the time hostility comes to fruition, he cannot even remember what its root is.

The desire to be special is man's problem; he has created his gods as a solution. In this plan, it is really the gods who make the selection; in this manner, the selection has divine authorship. Invariably, man is the one that is chosen. God is not involved or implicated by man's schemes. God is God; there is no other. The idea of specialness is totally meaningless. The thought that God could have a chosen people demonstrates ignorance, and such a doctrine is absurd; the premise is absolutely untenable.

When man chooses to remember God, he will have no need for specialness. When man decides to recall God, he will forget the falsity of chosenness. When he finally allows the knowledge of God (and there is no doubt that he must), man will have no more needs.

CHAPTER 13
God, the Warrior

In the midst of all the uncertainty of man's experience, two conditions or events are certain: death and war. The fabric of the traditions and customs of man is held together in the milieu of war. Man's existence would seem incomplete and unfulfilled without war.

The ultimate basis, in fact, the only basis of war is lack. It always seems to man that there is not enough of the desirable goods, whatever they are, to go around. Demand always appears to outstrip supply; the more the commodity is considered essential the less its availability.

Man's existence is largely dependent on supply-and-demand—with man demanding all the time from a limited supply. This situation accentuates the condition of lack; it is, therefore, not too difficult to deduce that the outcome is war in perpetuation. In essence, man's mode of existence invites war.

Man very quickly and easily justifies war and rationalizes it in various ways other than the real reason. There is an active repression of the real cause of war; there is a determined and concerted effort to ignore the underlying basis of war. A well-orchestrated conspiracy against the investigation of the true origins of war exists.

Man take his gods to war with him. In fact, he often claims that his gods commanded him to go to war. At other times, he claims that he is protecting his gods or defending his beliefs in these gods when he goes to war. Although he claims to wage war for ideological reasons, the basic motivation is the perceived need for limited resources.

Therefore, man goes to war with the name of his gods on his lips. He invokes the gods to prevail in his favor and deliver his enemies to him. He gives credit to his gods for his stamina in battle and courage. He imputes victory to those gods to whom he does obeisance. While dying from his battle wounds, he still honors his gods, either for solace or to celebrate martyrdom.

History is replete with the accounts of wars fought for man's gods or fought on man's behalf by his gods. History relates many accounts of man's romance with wartime martyrdom. His willingness and zealotry with regard to war are an eloquent statement of his understanding (or lack thereof) concerning the meaning of war.

Of all his reasons to engage in war, man's insistence on the support of his gods for war is the most pathetic. How else could one regard such rationalization, considering the destructiveness of war and the untold devastation? How else could one look upon such reasoning after seeing the misery and intense suffering caused by war? Who can bear the shame of the dehumanizing effects of war?

Gods who instigate or support war should be thoroughly ashamed of themselves; gods who fight battles and rape humanity in the name of war are totally depraved and owe the world an apology. Any god who enjoys the sight of maimed and crippled humanity and relishes the scream of terrified men, women, and children must be Mentally deranged.

These are the gods who savor the torturing of man and drool over the shedding of man's blood. They are at their best when the flesh of man burns in the inferno that is war. They are happiest when man falls a hapless victim to war; they are tickled when infants waste away in hunger, deprivation, and displacement from war.

Since their favorite spectacle is the squalor of refugee camps and the cruelty of concentration camps, these same gods make their beds on the piles of human bones and smashed skeletons that are the relics of war. Their music for relaxation consists of the blast of explosives and the grinding of human flesh against metal and dirt, the splatter of dismembered body parts on rocks, and the ominous whistle of missiles.

These, of course, are the gods who were created by man in the first place. They have no independent existence outside of man's mind: in fact, they have no existence at all except in the beliefs and customs of man. Man plays out his feelings and struggles and acts out his aggression arising from survival instincts, only to blame it on his gods. These same gods are believed to have been responsible for creating man.

Man gives God a bad name because there is no iota of divinity or even common dignity in the comportment or deportment of that creation man calls his gods. There is nothing godly about the gods of man, nothing sublime at all. To associate any gods with man is to seriously damage their reputation.

Man will continue to wage war until he gives up the conditions that spur war. When he does give up these conditions and the gods of his own creation, he will come to know God. God has nothing to do with war or with man or with any creation, for God is God: God knows only God. Man will accept this knowledge ultimately and man will no longer be—for only God is and will be.

CHAPTER 14
The Emotional God

Man is an emotional being. Without emotions, man is bland, lacking fire and zeal and style. Without emotions, man has no appeal, and life has no zest. Living would be missing from life; dullness would set in, and drive would be absent from the attributes of man.

The force of emotions has moved man's mountains when he needed to. When he otherwise could not be moved, the power of emotions has moved man. The strength of emotions has carried man to heights previously unattainable; the flavor of emotions has greatly embellished and even sweetened sour experiences for man.

Yet, the nature and origin of emotions continues to elude man. He must content himself with the attempt to master these emotions and, therefore, control them. Failing that, he must contend with the consequences of the wielding of a force which he has no control over; in fact, more often than not, he himself is under the control of this force and becomes an unwilling instrument of this unknown influence.

What better attributes to assign to his gods than his emotions! Emotions encompass the same qualities as man's gods—powerful, unknown, and inscrutable; their origins are unclear. Emotions are dangerous and constructive at the same time, very much like the dualistic nature of the gods. Emotions can be overpowering; so can the gods.

Man has thus ascribed to his gods such emotions as anger. Divine anger can and has done divine-sized damage—ask man! Was it not the anger of the gods that has resulted in the great calamities and so-called natural disasters in all epochs of human history, even at this moment? Surely, the world remains in business at this time not so much because it has found favor in the eyes of the gods as because the gods have mercifully shown restraint.

What about jealousy? Man's gods have plenty of that, too. If man ever thought of finding a different deity to serve and service, his jealous gods would fault him quickly and cut him down mercilessly wherever he stood. Nor would his gods spare him if they caught him nurturing the idea or practice of pantheism. Should man become so engrossed in other pursuits that he forgot his gods, that would be considered an act of infidelity and idolatry and would be quite punishable.

Even fear is imputed to man's gods—but in a very cautious manner. For example, in one popular version of the lores of man and his gods, the latter became afraid that man would find and eat "the fruit of the tree of life" and thereby achieve immortality. Of course the gods could not stand to see that; fearing the consequences, they took care of it before it could occur. Consider also the story of the origin of languages. Humanity had gathered as a community and built the Tower of Babel, an impressive accomplishment at the time. The only factor that made this possible was cooperation by human beings. Since all humanity was in agreement about something, an otherwise impossible task was completed (or more accurately, nearing completion). The gods panicked; insecure about the fact that man could become united in purpose and, therefore, unstoppable and invincible, the "confounded" man. Giving him different languages and dispersing him to various, remote corners of the world, they confused him. Never again could humanity be in agreement about anything; never again would humanity easily understand one another.

When they were not showing their own fear, man's gods were busy striking fear into the heart of timid man to keep him subdued, subjugated, and terrified. In this manner, man could never question them in challenge, nor could he find the courage to rebel against them.

Just like man, man's gods showed positive emotions, Just like man, such emotion was short-lived and in short supply. Such positive emotions had their dual opposites. Reckoning by human experience, the emotion that is more likely to be exhibited is the negative one.

There is no doubt that the emotions that man attributes to his gods are actually his. Whatever man's gods can do is actually determined by man. In fact, man's emotional set is the same as that of his gods, which is not surprising since the gods are a creation of man, though he chooses now to think otherwise.

God is who God is. God does not deal with emotions because emotions are not God. God has no emotions; God has only God because that is what God is. God is life and life is God; no spice or spark is missing or needed. Someday man will give up his emotions and their dualities, together with his emotional gods. At that time man will know God.

CHAPTER 15
The Inscrutable God

Man accepts the fact that he cannot have direct knowledge of his gods. In fact he prefers it that way. For man, true knowledge of a thing invites contempt. To know a thing is to denigrate it and to strip it of its mystique.

Man prefers that his gods be shrouded in insoluble mystery. He believes the process of knowing and knowledge itself corrupts the object in human hands. As man correctly put it, "familiarity breeds contempt."

When he applies the term *holy* to his gods, man really means to place them far apart, very far apart from knowledge by him. Man will stop at nothing to keep his gods at such a distance from himself. He will use every tactic available to obstruct any attempt to know his gods. Indeed, he has committed murder, perjury, and character assassination all in an effort to prevent attempts at gaining knowledge. He has meted out the most hideous cruelty and demonstrated unparalleled callousness to those seeking knowledge.

Instead of direct knowledge, man espouses faith. Ordinarily, faith is a quiet and firm reassurance that what is true remains true and immutable. As used by man and applied to his gods, faith becomes a veritable cover for inertia and resistance to enlightenment and knowledge. Faith becomes an excuse for not unwrapping layers of shrouds that obscure a mystery, the mystery that is man's gods. This adulterated version of faith protects a mystery but makes no statement about truth.

What dark secrets about his gods is man trying to protect? Is he perhaps afraid that beyond that holy veil is nothing—nothing more than man's own creation? Is man terrified at the prospects of penetrating that mysterious shroud only to face himself as its only substance?

Worried about the credibility and perpetuation of his gods, man is eager to cover up truth and oppose and ignore knowledge. He is more concerned about maintaining the mystique of his gods than he is of facing reality. His only goal—his only priority—is to protect his gods at all costs.

Fortunately, ignorance is not tolerated forever. Fortunately, there is a cadre of humanity that is seriously and diligently pursuing knowledge; it will carve a path through the mysterious province of man's gods. This section of humanity constitutes the faithful because they are convinced that truth remains true, knowable, and attainable.

One hopes the march of knowledge will not terminate at the demystification of the gods of man. It is quite certain (though it may not seem so at the time) that man will discover that the gods whom he has worshipped all these days are objects of his creation. That discovery by itself should not and will not be the end of the quest for knowledge. It should serve as an impetus to know what lies ahead; it will serve as a new beginning in the direction that is man's ultimate destiny.

God is very knowable, and man will know God. Inscrutability is not of God; it is not God. Why would God hide Himself, and from whom? God is neither mysterious nor steeped in mystique. God has no thought or need of protection from knowledge. God remains God and is incorruptible and not subject to tarnishment because He is known. God neither reveals nor is God to be revealed because God was never hidden or inaccessible in the first place.

In time, man will abandon his secretive ways and face the empty mysteries that he has built up. Then, he will dismiss them. Then, he will want to know again what he had previously chosen to hide from, what he previously had tried so hard to ignore and neglect. Here at last man will know God.

CHAPTER 16
The Temple of God

To preserve the holiness of his gods, man has always protected them from general access. It makes no difference whether such access is in the form of mental knowledge or that of a more concrete physical nature.

The gods of man are thus enshrined in temples and, in some cases, breath-taking edifices. By custom, these buildings are considered sacred and are generally out of bounds to man except under certain circumstances and during certain periods. For here reside the gods, and they must be revered and not disturbed.

The cost in human labor and resources to erect these architectural masterpieces is staggering; in general, the price is unknown. Usually man does not bother to ask; he has been taught not to question anything he does in the name of his gods. (Unless, of course, he is part of the forced labor necessary to built these temples in times past and present; in that case, questioning would bring only one answer—torture, rape, and death.)

Within these temples man formalizes, codifies, and consummates his relationship with his gods in ceremony and rituals. Here he is obligated to pay homage with typical posturation to his gods in a timely and regular fashion, failing which, the ire of the gods would be aroused. In that instance, the consequences would be severe; retribution would be swift and drastic.

Outside the gorgeous buildings, humanity wallows in abject poverty and languishes in homelessness. Yet, being so devout, it would give its last resource to support the prodigious budget of the temples. Humanity would expend her last breath in utterance of some supplication to these gods. It would tire from the maintenance of the temples before it could even manage its own tattered affairs.

Man's gods love the glitter of silver and the azure of diamonds; they love the look of gold and the precious metals and trinkets with which their temples are adorned. They relish the gilded and polished furnishings, the lavish decorations. They never seem satisfied; they are just as eager to accept, or more correctly, extract more and more—each and every time. Man is not bothered by this because he thinks that his gods deserve everything without exception.

What kind of a god can reside with pride and in comfort in a home built out of rocks and gems? Obviously such a god does not care for permanence and durability because rocks crumble with regularity and gems tarnish with predictability. Perhaps such a god does not really consider it a problem since he knows that his human subjects will gladly maintain the upkeep of his home at all costs (to mankind, of course).

More important, it must be an insensitive god who makes his temple a place that is built, literally, with human blood and sweat. What is the body-count of the casualties who died needlessly in forced labor or in martyrdom just to provide this building for the god? It must be a greedy god who expects or demands his subjects' last farthing, so that he can add to his collection of ornaments. Yet, it is common knowledge that the temples remain empty without the bustle of deities living there; the only warmth is provided by periodic human activity. The same fate that is the lot of mundane buildings becomes the fate of all temples. None of the gems or ornaments will ever be worn or used by any god or gods; the gods will never touch the money that comes from alms and tithing.

Meanwhile, the homeless brave the vagaries of a hostile climate with no hope for shelter. The hungry still go hungry though food could be provided for some at little cost. The poor might improve their lot, but they are impoverished even more by the customary taxing in the name of man's gods.

Similar conditions have provoked social revolutions in the history of mankind. They will force man eventually to re-evaluate his relationship with his gods. They will compel him to re-examine the nature of his gods. These conditions will scream the question, "Who are these gods?"

Sooner or later, man will ask and then truthfully answer that question. When that happens, he will admit that he created these gods himself; he will then realize that he has no need for them. He will also realize that he has no need to create anything because he will know God. God has no temple; God requires no temple.

CHAPTER 17
Relating to God

Relating to his gods is an act that is performed in carefully stipulated ways by man. The stipulation is presumably authored by the gods and handed to messengers or agents of the gods. From here, the information in the form of commands or commandments is passed on to representatives of the faithful who then translate them into doctrine and dogma. Using whatever means appear effective, this code is next disseminated to the laity.

The manner in which man relates to his gods is quite interesting. First, it is done with the presumption of a hierarchical order in which the gods are obviously far above and beyond man. At man's level are other sublevels providing for a wide range of posts and functions. Often the lowest echelon is not permitted direct access to the gods without intercession by a higher rank.

Second, it is mostly a lop-sided relationship in which the gods have all the aces, so to speak. Man must beg for their tender mercies. Though he chooses to call it prayer or supplication, man's intonation and comportment betray his real act of pure mendicancy.

The third interesting aspect of man's relationship to his gods is communication. Of the two parties, man communicates more clearly, more vocally, and with a more contemporary symbolism than his gods. In fact the intent and meaning of his god's communication are usually subject to interpretation. Attempts to literally follow the communications of the gods have always proven impractical and have failed to eliminate the intrinsic ambiguity that characterizes them.

To qualify for the gods' blessings, man must worship and love them. The requisite rites and rituals of worship are really not suited for the fragile skeleton of man; the gods should know that—they are credited with creating man. Nor are they suited to man's ego. Basically, man would have to humble himself to be eligible for what his gods have to dole out. As a matter of fact, there is no line between humility and humiliation when it comes to the worship of the gods.

What about love? It is required that man love his gods. Consider that man does not and cannot even love himself or his fellow man. How could he show love when he does not even know what love is? And even if he could, how could he in all honesty show true love to his gods when he knows that a cruel punishment surely awaits him if he does not?

Naturally, man should learn love from his gods who are supposed to have made him in their own image, but man's relationship with his gods is too dominated by fear and intimidation to allow for any lessons in love. After all, these are the gods who have no qualms about the destruction of the world. These are the same gods who take sides in wars and aid one party in the massacre of the other. These are the gods in whose name and by whose authority the most hideous atrocities are committed by mankind.

Where is the love of the gods when the gods rain disease and illness on helpless subjects? Where is their love when heartbreak and heartache are routine experiences among their people? They would cause man to die and rot after his flesh is wasted by famine and sickness. Is this love?

Yet, they demand that man love them. How is that possible? Poor man! He tries, oh how hard he tries! But he has to—the consequences are severe. In reality, it is the fear and anticipation rather than the retribution itself that cripples man because there is no new hurt. He has already been hurt in every way possible; he has already been hurt in unimaginable places.

If the gods of man were real, man would certainly be in perpetual danger due to their great propensity to hurt him. Fortunately, these gods exist only in the belief of man and have no independent substance or essence. Since they are the product of man's machinations, they reflect man's character except that they are beyond challenge and reproach, unlike man himself.

Man created his gods in his own image and clothed them with his ideas of divinity, but his ideas of divinity are severely limited by what man can conceive, The ideas are defined by man's repertoire of symbolism. Whatever man can do, his gods can do too—no more, no less,

God has no relationship with man; God is God and only relates to God. The thought of worship is not of God or from God; there is no element or symbolism in worship that applies or appeals to God. God asks nothing of anyone because God needs nothing of anyone. Man will come to know God when he has tired of his preoccupation with the things that he has created. There is no question but that such a time must come.

CHAPTER 18
God's Blessings

To his gods, man very quickly credits happy events and windfalls; these are otherwise called blessings. They are considered gifts from benevolent gods to needy, worthy, and deserving underlings.

Blessings come in various forms. The most valued are life, health, food, offspring, and wealth. Man spends a lot of prayer-time asking for these. He also spends a lot of time and energy thanking his gods for such blessings.

Man feels that the blessings of his gods will continue to flow if he shows appreciation. As such, he has devised many rituals and ceremonies to honor his gods for their kindness and thereby ensure more blessings.

Such rituals include tithing, alms-giving, and so-called burnt offerings. Such rituals involve sacrificial acts that often jeopardize life and property. As a sign of thanksgiving, they sometimes demand giving back some or all of the blessings to the gods.

Yet, none of the blessings from man's gods comes free of charge or as a straightforward source of joy. In fact, they are merely the other side of a system of duality; they have no virtual meaning except in contradistinction and by comparison.

Consider the most supreme of the blessings of man's gods—life. This tenuous existence often lived at the expense of someone else's life will, sooner or later, always end in death, that most feared of all the destinies of mankind. If everything is a blessing, then life is quickly overwhelmed by the more dramatic and terminal bane that is death. What a blessing!

It is interesting that health is considered a blessing from the gods. A divine gift should be more permanent and reliable. Good health is neither permanent nor reliable in the experience of man; it is as unstable as earth's weather. While man is known to work very hard to sustain good health, it is a truly uphill battle that has only one outcome. That outcome is always on the side against health,

Food is another example of the blessings of man's gods. Yet, food does not drop on man as manna from heaven, for man has to work for it, and very hard too. Often, all the hard work is for nothing because the yield of food falls far too short of the demand. What is considered the blessing of food for man is often the horrible fact of death for another species.

Man considers the ability for procreation a blessing, but the process of parturition is a most painful experience for the female of the species and the baby itself, In these days, the process is an impoverishing event that often leaves all parties concerned without sufficient means for succor. Even Mother Earth is now threatened by the serious possibility of overpopulation.

It is not entirely clear why a benevolent god would ask for something in return for his blessings, whatever such blessings are. Man teaches that his gods do expect something back, whether it be the simple act of thanksgiving and worship or the actual sacrifice of something organic or inorganic. He practices this teaching with diligence. A god who asks for something needs something; a god that needs something is not perfect. If giving is at all feasible. such a god or gods would give imperfect gifts but only in exchange for their own needs. Yes, these are the gods who will always take more than they give because man's needs are puny compared to the needs of his all-powerful gods.

Man's gods are very much like man—very needy, very insatiable. Like man, they are not really benevolent; they give only on the condition that they are paid back with greedy interest. It is an unfair exchange rate, and there is nothing blessed about their transactions.

It really is no surprise that man's gods are like him. He created them, after all, though he tries so hard to teach and believe otherwise. Man did create his gods in his likeness; their qualities are no more and no less than man's.

Beyond man's relationship with his gods is God. God remains God, and the knowledge of Him awaits man with a certain destiny. At such a time that man lets go of his own creations, he will fulfill this destiny. And he certainly will!

CHAPTER 19
God's Commandments

The need for order is a real part of the life of man. Without order, life has a natural tendency towards chaos. It took no time for man to realize this; the fact that science only recently (in relative terms) formalized this tendency as the law of entropy is not impressive. Man has always known this in his experience.

Order is imposed at the cost of power; therefore, a powerful authority is essential for the establishment of order in any system, Neither the authority nor its power need be real as long as the perception is present. In other words, only a belief in the existence of the authority and in the power of such an authority is necessary. To maintain this state of affairs, it becomes necessary that the authority not be challenged and its power not be contested.

Since entropy is universal, the authority for order has to have universal appeal. A local power that has no influence on the rest of the world could not survive and will not suffice. This removes the authority from the grasp of man, he is just too "local" to be capable of wielding such power.

It is, therefore, not surprising that man assigned the authority and authorship of order to his gods. The power also was given to the gods by man, for only the gods have the know-how and the stamina to maintain order in the universe.

Man was not, however, left out of the picture in this business. He is sometimes appointed to be the police and sometimes the messenger of the gods for this purpose. Mostly, he is the instrument by which this order will be maintained. He bears the responsibility of behaving himself and comporting himself in a manner in which order is maintained.

The commandments (and there are many of them) are the rules given by man's gods specifically for the purpose of maintaining order. The commandments also spell out the way man should treat his gods in order to keep them happy. Some commandments specify the punishment for lack of adherence to the rules.

Common to most commandments are the concepts of recognition of the gods, love, and life. Usually, the charge is to love and worship the gods and then to love others and oneself. Man is instructed to respect life and not kill. These are, of course, all honorable ideas and concepts.

However, if these are the commandments of the gods, then the gods themselves, along with man, are breaking most of them. The gods ask man not to kill; however, they created man to be dependent on flesh for survival—be it the flesh of less fortunate species or even that of the same species. Even when he feeds on vegetables, he still kills to survive, thanks to his designer.

In times of war, man takes his gods along with him, if they did not order and declare the war in the first place. He invokes the help of his gods to kill his enemies; of course, the gods readily oblige (assuming that the gods did not strike the first blow themselves). Yet, the gods commanded, "Thou shalt not kill."

In the event of the accidental or natural death of man, it is not unusual for man to assume that since his gods gave him life in the first place, they can later take it back. It is not just an assumption; it is a fact of man's beliefs and his relationship to his gods. If the gods take away man's life, then the gods have killed. Judging from experience and actuaries, the gods are doing a lot of killing.

The hypocrisy of man's gods cannot be exposed any deeper than when one contemplates the idea of love. First, they command man to love them. If man assumes that birth is the first event in his life, then right there and then the gods start showing him anything but love. The pain and suffering and trauma of parturition, the precariousness of the birth process, and the uncertainty of the outcome are cruel facts of obstetrics. The newborn infant makes it not because of the gods but in spite of them; the same statement applies to the mother.

If death is the last event of man's life, how does that demonstrate his gods' love for him? Where is the glory and joy in dying to qualify death as an act of love? Here again, the act of love by man's gods cannot be detected.

From birth to death, there is little to objectify the demonstration of love by the gods of man. What little love that is presumed by man is quickly overshadowed by the two most dramatic events in man's life The gods of man demand man's love; they themselves show no love, but man keeps trying to love them anyway.

Man also keeps trying to love his fellow man the best way he knows how, but he hurts his fellow man, competes with him, duels with him, exploits him, and hates him—all in the name of love. Having learned from his gods, he has emulated them in every way.

Man's gods do not deserve love because they have no more knowledge of what love is than does man. All the commandments attributed to the gods are laws of man made by man for man. Man has great needs that must be filled; he will fill them the best way he knows how. That's why he will also try to use the gods (whom he created) as an authority for the purpose of extracting compliance from his fellow man.

While engaged as such, man is too preoccupied to notice the presence of God. Man will yet exhaust himself in the futility of his own engrossment in the fruitlessness of his own fixations. Then, it will happen—he will know God. He must.

CHAPTER 20
The Gender of God

However it came about, the masculine gender has become the dominant sex of the human species. This dominance is so entrenched in some cultures that the female gender cannot be recognized in public. More sad than this state of affairs is the fact that it is accepted unquestionably by both men and woman.

Typically, man attributes the establishment of gender to his gods. Gender is presumed necessary for procreation and for companionship—never mind that reproduction can be accomplished without different sexes and that companionship is possible without the invocation of a different sex. In fact, satisfying companionship does not even have to be sexual.

As one would expect from his anthropocentricity and chauvinism, man identifies his gods with the dominant sex of the human species, They have to be male; their qualities and attributes have to be unequivocally masculine, complete with phallic symbolism.

The female has become a second-class citizen in the human race and, in some places, a "noncitizen" all because the gods ordained it. In their divine wisdom, the gods decided that the female is inferior; the male, in obedience to the instructions of his gods, will enforce this decision.

So strong is the male conviction about the god-determined status of the female that he denies her the right to participate in any important role in the rituals of worship or service of man's gods. Often, she may not even be allowed a voice in the decision-making process.

Fortunately, man's thinking is changing some. In fact, he did make some of his gods female and assigned typically feminine responsibilities to them. Although within divine circles, the female deity is to the male deity what a woman is to man in human terms, in some places, the female can serve the gods of man in similar circumstances and with equal rank as the male.

The defense of gender dominance on grounds of divine endowment is illogical; in fact, the defense of gender dominance on any grounds is totally illogical. Man only exposes his ignorance and the weaknesses of his gods by his insistence on gender dominance.

Today, with the use of the right hormones, the skill of a surgeon so inclined, and the acquisition of the right mannerisms, gender becomes almost one hundred percent exchangeable. In the future, medical science will have the ability to inject or delete the X or Y chromosome into the embryo so that one can choose and control the gender of the yet-to-be-born infant.

Today, the stereotypical gender roles are fast disappearing in some societies as man realizes that roles are learned and are interchangeable. Few (if any) anatomical barriers affecting functionality exist whose limitations cannot be overcome directly or indirectly.

Even the usual reasons for gender differences and hierarchies have given way to the realities, practices, and practicalities of the times. The most natural and traditional reasons have not been spared either. Consider that a baby can be made and grown without intercourse and that man can choose which of several embryos can be nurtured. The day is not too far in the future when the female will be completely relieved of the burden of pregnancy if she so chooses, as fetuses are grown in artificial culture mediums.

The role of gender in sexuality is changing, too. Whether in the sense of a physical and emotional act or in the esoteric sense of the wielding of the power of so-called creative energy, there is no requirement for having opposite sexes in order for man to experience sexual pleasures.

In fact, if current trends continue, man may only need a machine or just his own thoughts alone to duplicate a perfect sexual experience; the presence of another human being could be superfluous.

As for the mystical creative energy of sexuality, that mystery is gone. Without the traditionally associated orgasmic moan and other psychic experiences of sexual intercourse, life can still be created in the laboratories. The sterile laboratories and the messy bedrooms now have something in common: they both can be in this energy field, and they both can generate this energy field. In addition, neither gender nor gender dominance is a requisite for their operations.

Needless to say, it is difficult for man to accept these developments. His allegiance to his gods is obviously threatened as much as the authority of his gods. The wisdom of his gods in creating different and hierarchical genders is being seriously questioned, and his assumed rationale for genders is being eroded. He reacts in a typical fashion; he becomes atavistic, digs in, and assumes a defensive mode by attacking and denigrating opposite views.

It would take man to invent gender dominance; it would take man's creation in the nature of his gods to support it. Who but man's gods (man's ideas in the first place) could discriminate the human species by gender? Who else would make his gods male because he is of the male gender?

The concept of gender has no meaning within the context of God. The idea of gender is totally meaningless in the knowledge of God. The issue of dominance is nonexistent in God or with God. This is the knowledge that awaits man; it will be there for him when he disengages himself from such concepts and issues.

CHAPTER 21
Man, the Agnostic

Man's attitude towards knowledge is basically negative, even antagonistic. To him, the pursuit of knowledge is essentially painful, a sacrifice. It is an exercise that he does not undertake with any alacrity because his default position is characterized by inertia, and his reaction to knowledge by fear.

Knowledge, a dirty word! According to the lore of man, it was the pursuit of knowledge that led to the downfall of man. He took the rest of creation down with him. For that effrontery, the gods branded him a sinner; only his death could atone for this fault. The gods were quite angered; the punishment meted to man was harsh, swift, and final.

The tradition of man demands that knowledge be regarded with fear and suspicion. Better still, "ignorance is bliss," a bliss that man has welcomed unabashedly, an ignorance that man has willingly accepted without hesitation or equivocation.

Indeed, knowledge can be destabilizing. The unknown gives no inkling of what it holds in store; it could be bad, or it could be very, very bad. Whether it holds the key to states that man had no idea how to cope with or it opens the doors to states where man had little or no power, once open, such doors could probably never be closed again. the consequences are frightening.

For whatever reason that man is afraid of knowledge, the fact still remains that he cannot get away from the compelling power to seek knowledge. Indeed, that power is irresistible to man because man's survival depends on knowledge. Often, the exhilaration resulting from the forbidden fruit of knowledge is much more stimulating and rewarding than the benefits, comforts, and security of the status quo. Yet, this last fact pales in the light of the need and drive for survival and existence.

Though reluctant, man has to seek knowledge; in a way, he has no choice. The results of his search have been spectacular. They have confirmed his worst fears in some areas, but they have also saved him in other areas. All in all, it's been a positive balance, but man is compelled to search more. For the more man knows, the more there is to know, and the more he wants to know.

Enter man's gods. They are not happy that man is seeking knowledge and are not amused by man's new initiative. In the beginning, in Eden, they were not amused; they are not happy now either. Man was made to be sorry then, and he will be even sorrier now. How dare man think that his survival is dependent on knowledge rather than on the benevolence of the gods?

In the fear of possible reprisal by his gods, man has clearly drawn the line of the boundaries of his search for knowledge. It precludes the gods and their domain. He will explore the earth and the sky; he will learn about anatomy and physiology, cosmology, and quantum physics. He will scrutinize and peer into the atom to pry its secrets, but somehow he will not ask the following questions: "Who are you, God?," "What is your nature?," and "What is my relationship to you?"

Man is the original agnostic because he believes that his gods are inscrutable. If they are inscrutable, then the gods cannot be known. Yes, man's gods are unknowable because man is afraid that their ire will be aroused once again if an attempt is made to find out about them. He is still reeling from the effects of the so-called original sin.

Of all the reasons advanced by man about why his gods cannot be known, the most curious one states that man could not fathom the knowledge of his gods. (At least an honest attempt could have been made to demonstrate this point.) It does seem logical that if he is made in the image of his gods, as man claims and teaches, he at least should have partial knowledge of those gods.

Maybe man does not indeed want to know his gods because they would not stand up to scrutiny. Maybe the lore and tradition of Eden is an excuse behind which man hides the truth of his gods—that they are a fabrication that he has cooked up and guarded closely and viciously.

It well may be that the agnostic indeed is no more. It well may be that man now knows his gods but is not ready or willing to admit it. Yes, man knows. Man knows himself; therefore, he knows his gods. His reluctance to know the gods of his own creation is actually a reluctance to know himself, for "like man, like his gods."

Man is truly afraid to know himself. The extent to which he knows himself is the extent to which he understands the gods whom he has made. What he has found so far is neither pleasing nor flattering. It is so disturbing that he does not want to continue to look. He is not very eager to continue his search.

Irrespective of the assumptions of man, God is fully knowable. God is the meaning of knowledge; knowledge describes no other than God and defines nothing other than God. There is neither fear in knowledge nor fear in God. Knowledge has no boundaries because God has no boundaries. Man will break the walls of the phobia of knowledge after wrestling and conquering his gods. The knowledge of God then becomes his experience. Nothing more awaits man.

CHAPTER 22
God and the Atheist

In the beginning, as the tradition goes, the gods created the earth and the world including man whom they made in their image. The gods created a wife (more like a companion or even a slave) for man. Every other creature was handed over to man for slaughter for food or game or pleasure. Soon thereafter, man became ambitious and tried to have knowledge; this greatly upset the gods. As punishment, the gods sacked man from Eden and cursed him for life, by instituting death for man as well as labor at work and at childbirth.

The gods demanded service and worship and love from man while they practically teased him with a few mixed blessings. For the sweet and sour blessings man was still required to give back something to the gods as an expression of appreciation. All the gods' demands were backed up by threats of divine reprisals and repercussions should their demands not be met.

While the gods spoke about love, they had no second thoughts about punishing man at will not about taking sides with one party against the other even when this resulted in the death of the other party. Nepotism and favoritism were practiced by the gods without regard to fairness. Neither do the gods show any discretion or sensitivity when they watch man writhe in pain and rot away as they take his life away from him.

It is not surprising that atheism should flourish. No clear thinking man would justify the actions or defend the character of these gods. Nobody with even the most elementary sense of fairness or the faintest hint of love and caring would want to be associated with these gods.

What is most surprising is that the proportion of those who do not believe in these gods is not higher that it is now. Without challenge, man continues to accept the nature and acts of his gods. Man will not let his fellow man get away with a minor infraction; yet, he accepts the murderous habits of his gods.

Atheism is a totally justified and quite understandable statement about gods who thrive on the misfortune of man. It demonstrates a comprehension of the fact that man's gods have no divinity at all. It is a courageous stance that is based on a simple understanding that man's gods are wicked and nefarious and do not deserve the adulation that they demand.

The gods of man are just that—man-made. To believe in them is to belief in man's creation. For man to hand over the control of his existence and his destiny to these gods is to shirk his responsibilities. He would be burying his head in the sand in the proverbial sense. As it were.

Man makes excuses for his gods in the same manner that a weakling would make excuses for a bully and for the same reasons, too. He is so afraid that his gods would get angry at him and smite him that he is very accommodating. Going out of his way to please and placate them in all circumstances, man continues to rationalize illogical behaviour and action on the part of his gods.

Man's dealings with his gods reveal a pathological relationship in which man is always the victim. It is reminiscent of typical pathological relationships that also exist in the world between human beings. Such relationships are characterized by roles in which the victims are always victimized, the predators are constantly preying on their victims, and both parties accept the relationship without question.

It is a moral obligation to question the relationship between man and his gods; it is a moral obligation to reject that relationship as it is now. Moreover, it is a logical step to dismiss the gods of man because they are entirely made up by man. Atheism is not a rebellion against the tradition of man and his gods; atheism is an honest expression of the fact that the gods of man have no existence of their own. It is a decision to dismiss such gods in act and in practice.

Today, man is divided concerning this issue. There are those that cling tenaciously to man's gods and defend their stance with strength, vigor, the blood of martyrdom, and their opponent's blood. There are those who believe in a new version of man's gods, a version upgraded to accommodate new facts and knowledge without terribly upsetting the basic tenets of the tradition of man's gods. There are yet those who don't really care and realize that they can get along just fine without addressing the issue of the gods of man. There are others who do not want anything to do with ineffectual gods; they are so-called atheists.

The battle will rage for a while as man expresses his allegiance and fights for his stance. Man will try to defend his tradition against those who attempt to change it or those that try to reject it. Meanwhile, the nonconformists will fight to retain their independence and their right of dissent.

When the dust settles from this ferocious fight, God will be evident; God has always been there. When the din of this raging battle dies down, God will be heard. After the war has exhausted itself, and the heat of battle has dissipated, the cool serenity of the peace that is God will be felt by man. Here at last man will know God; now at last man will have knowledge of God. That is an event that will not fail to occur. To know God is the only destiny of man.

Epilogue

What He or She is,
God,
Man yet has to know;
God, by man
made and created
He or She is not.

Who He or She is,
God,
Man will yet discover;
God, of Man
conceived and fashioned,
He or She is not.

How He or She is,
God,
Man is soon to feel;
God, in man's image
cast and molded,
He or She is not.

Where He or She is,
God,
Man is yet to be;
God, by man
placed and postured,
He or She is not.

God always is
God,
Man must find out;
God, to man
finally revealed
He or She is.

God still is
God;
Man's happy fate 'tis
God to man
to be known in full
Who He or She is.

www.ingramcontent.com/pod-product-compliance
Lightning Source LLC
Chambersburg PA
CBHW061714120626
46550CB00003B/1218